The Girl's Guide to

WIZARDS

Everything Magical about
These Spellbinders

by Jen Jones

CAPSTONE PRESS
a capstone imprint

Snap Books are published by Capstone Press,
151 Good Counsel Drive, P.O. Box 669, Mankato, Minnesota 56002.
www.capstonepub.com

Books published by Capstone Press are manufactured with paper
containing at least 10 percent post-consumer waste.

Library of Congress Cataloging-in-Publication Data
Jones, Jen.
  The girl's guide to wizards : everything magical about these spellbinders.
    p. cm. — (Snap)
  Summary: "Describes the mystery, cool characteristics, and allure of wizards, including historical and
contemporary examples"—Provided by publisher.
  ISBN 978-1-4296-5454-8 (library binding)
  1. Wizards—Juvenile literature. I. Title.
  BF1611.J66 2011
  133.4'3—dc22   2010037843

Editorial Credits

Editors: Kathryn Clay
Designer: Tracy Davies
Media Researcher: Marcie Spence
Production Specialist: Laura Manthe

Photo Credits:

123RF: Ben Heys, 23, Karen Struthers, 27 (bottom); Alamy: Illustration Works/Doug Gray, 4, Photos 12, 28 (bottom);
Capstone Press: 11 (all), 12 (all); Getty Images Inc.: AFP, 8, APIC, 29 (top), Eric Charbonneau/WireImage, 29 (middle),
Eric McCandless/Disney Channel, 28 (middle), TimePix/Time Life Pictures, 29 (bottom); Globe Photos: 18; Newscom:
Bob D'Amico/Disney Channel/MCT, 7, DDP/Michael Urban, 15 (middle), SHNS photo curtesy of Warner Brothers,
27 (middle), Walt Disney Pictures/Bray, Phil, 27 (top), Warner Bros. Pictures, 28 (top); Shutterstock: Alexandru Axon,
17 (bottom), Anyka, 14, argus, cover (star), buruhtan, 17 (top), gregg Williams, 22, hfng, 15 (bottom), Kudryashka,
cover (book), LilKar, 20, Nick Biemans, 21, OnFocus, cover (girl silhouette), Scott Rothstein, 17 (middle), Stakhiv
Arsen Ivanovich, 16, Subbotina Anna, cover (background), Vinicius Tupinamba, 15 (top), Vladimir Prusakov, 5, Vlue,
cover (wand).

Printed in the United States of America in North Mankato, Minnesota.
092010
005933CGS11

Contents

Chapter One

The Wonderful World of Wizardry

Ever wish you could make something happen with a simple wave of a wand? Welcome to the wonderful and sometimes wacky world of wizards. Here, anything is possible. No cheesy card tricks or hat-dwelling rabbits allowed.

The magic of wizards goes far beyond that of your average magician. Wizard powers often come from within. In fact, the name comes from the Old English word *wysard*, which means "wise one." Wizards use their smarts to create spells, curses, and potions.

Wizards are also known as warlocks. Female wizards can also be known as witches.

Get ready to meet some of the most memorable fantasy figures in history and pop culture. Plus, you'll learn the secrets behind wizard magic. Soon you'll see why fantasy just wouldn't be the same without these marvelous magicians.

What secrets could this witch be hiding?

WHERE WIZARDS COME FROM

According to legends, wizards are all around us. Yet most people outside the wizarding world never know it. Many **mortals** don't believe magic is real. They think spells are made for fiction and fairy tales. And wizards are just fine with that. After all, the world of wizards is top secret. Thanks to special powers and potions, anything can happen. The less mortals know, the better.

How does one get a ticket to this mysterious world? Well, it's not easy. Most wizards are born, not made. Just look at Hogwarts School of Witchcraft and Wizardry in the Harry Potter series. Most Hogwarts students get their magic talent from their parents. Only a few "outsiders" are born with magic. But at the Unseen University in the Discworld series, older wizards are there to introduce younger ones to the world of magic.

mortal: someone or something that is not able to live forever; humans are mortal

Sometimes young wizards become **apprentices**, like Alex Russo on the show *Wizards of Waverly Place*. Alex and her siblings, Max and Justin, carefully study under their wizard parents. When the Russos become adults, they will have a contest to see which one is the best wizard. The winner gets to keep his or her powers. The losers turn into mortals. Whichever path one takes to become a wizard, there's sure to be a lot of hard work along the way.

The cast of *Wizards of Waverly Place*

apprentice: someone who learns a trade or craft by working with a skilled person

BEHIND THE CURTAIN

With all this power at their fingertips, wizards must choose how to use it. Many wizards use their magic for good. Master wizards, like Harry Potter's headmaster Albus Dumbledore, use their powers to teach. Young wizards must learn to use magic properly. Ged Sparrowhawk, the main character in *A Wizard of Earthsea*, is sent to wizarding school. He needs to learn how to control his powers to avoid hurting himself and others.

Albus Dumbledore

Other wizards choose to use dark magic. In some cases, good wizards must spend all their time and energy stopping the plans of evil wizards. Lord Voldemort in the Harry Potter series is a perfect example. Harry spends seven years fighting the Dark Lord. Whether good or evil magic is being practiced, there is rarely a dull moment in the wizarding world!

Wizards, both good and evil, have been around for thousands of years.

Ancient tales tell of **shamans** and magicians. Wise people were often considered to be wizards in villages and royal courts during the 1400s. Even the ancient Roman poet Virgil may have been a wizard. Many people believed his writings had hidden meanings and future **predictions**. These early mystics paved the way for the wizards of today.

shaman: a religious leader who uses magic

prediction: a statement of what you think will happen in the future

FOLLOW the FANTASY
PAGE-TURNING READS

Fictional wizards often work their magic on readers. Both teens and adults have fallen for the idea of a magical world. Many books have been so popular that they've been turned into multi-book series.

 READ IT: Young Wizards (series) by Diane Duane

Follow the adventures of wizard BFFs Nita and Kit. The pair joins forces against bullies and other creepy creatures. Set on the streets of Manhattan, these books show a whole new side to the city that never sleeps.

 READ IT: Harry Potter (series) by J. K. Rowling

With seven books, this series sat on the *New York Time's* bestseller list for 10 years. The final book, *Harry Potter and the Deathly Hallows*, sold more than 8 million copies on the first day! Enter the hallowed halls of Hogwarts School of Witchcraft and Wizardry. Then find out why Harry, Ron, Hermione, and Dumbledore have become household names.

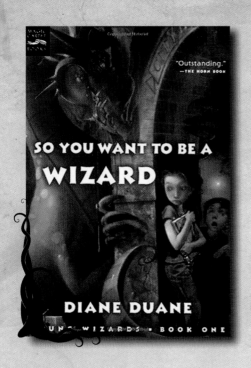

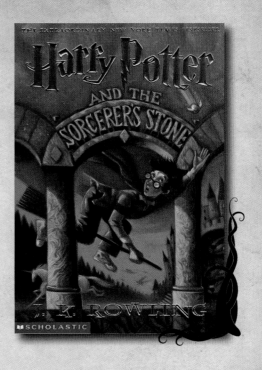

READ IT: Wizards of Skyhall (series) by J. R. King

The books' heroine, Arianna Kelt, isn't a wizard. But she can see wizards. This special skill creates all kinds of problems for the wizards of Skyhall. They are supposed to keep the secret of wizards' existence from humans. What's the most amazing part of these books? The author was just 12 years old when he wrote them.

FOLLOW the FANTASY ON SCREEN

The world of wizards isn't just for readers. Many magic makers have made their way to the screen as well.

WATCH IT: *Wizards of Waverly Place, The Movie*

Based on the Disney show, this 2009 movie followed the Russo family to Hawaii. Selena Gomez, David Henrie, and Jake T. Austin star as siblings who are wizards-in-training. Things get tricky when Alex (Selena) wishes her parents had never met. She quickly learns to be careful about what you wish. To fix things, the kids must use magic and find the Stone of Dreams. Otherwise, their family could disappear forever.

WATCH IT: Harry Potter (series)

When these best-selling books went to Hollywood, fans flocked to see the Hogwarts gang on the big screen. The movies are packed with jaw-dropping special effects and fast-paced action. The final book, *Harry Potter and the Deathly Hallows*, has been split into two feature length movies. Fans were sad to see their beloved series end, but happy to get a double dose of their favorite wizard.

WATCH IT: The Lord of the Rings (series)

Before becoming a fan favorite on the big screen, The Lord of the Rings was a classic **trilogy**. Author J. R. R. Tolkien introduced audiences to a world filled with hobbits, wizards, and elves. And who could forget Gandalf the Grey?

trilogy: a series of three works that are closely related

Chapter Two

Styles and Sidekicks

Wizardly Wear

When you imagine wizards, you probably picture long beards, dark cloaks, and pointy hats. But like people, wizards come in all shapes, ages, sizes, and styles. Some even prefer to dress like mortals. No matter their level of passion for fashion, here are a few must-haves for any wizard wardrobe.

Robes: Long, magical robes can do amazing things. They might make a wizard invisible. They may keep a wizard safe from danger. You can learn a lot about wizards just by looking at the color of their robes. A purple robe stands for knowledge. A white robe shows protective powers. Robes also mark the difference between good and evil wizards. The good wear white, while the bad wear black.

Hats: A wizard's hat can be decorated with symbols like suns, moons, and stars. Some symbols have secret meanings, like a wizard's real name. In the Harry Potter series, the Sorting Hat decides students' houses at Hogwarts. It also warns Harry of future dangers in his fight against Voldemort.

Rings: When a wizard accessorizes, it's not just for looks. Rings are often sources of great power. Just think of the One Ring in The Lord of the Rings. Whoever dared to wear the gold band could become invisible or even take over the world!

Wands and staffs: Many wizards carry tall staffs or short wands. Staffs are usually made of wood from an enchanted tree. Wizards store magic inside the staffs to use in times of need. Wands are different because magic travels through them. Wizards use the wands to stir potions and cast spells.

Familiars: Many wizards have faithful "familiars" by their side. Familiars are loyal pets that help wizards with spells. They can also spy and deliver special messages. The Halliwell sisters' familiar was a cat on the TV series *Charmed*.

Chapter Three

Under the Spell

Wizardly Skills

Speaking with animals is just one of many cool things that wizards do. They can also make objects fly or create fire from thin air. All of these incredible acts are everyday happenings for wizards. The magic often becomes even stronger the longer wizards practice. Here's a short list of wizard skills.

Cast spells: Have you ever said "abracadabra", "hocus pocus", or "presto chango"? Well, guess what? You were casting a spell! Wizards can cast spells easily. To create this magic, wizards say spells using poems, rhymes, and songs.

Mix potions: Wizards have the power to whip up some seriously strong potions. These bewitching brews can make a person fall in love. They can also change a person's age or appearance. Some potions can even heal wounds. From frog toes and candle wax to pixie dust, it's anyone's guess what ends up in the mix. Some ingredients are hard to find, but the results are well worth the hunt.

Mind tricks: With the aid of **illusions**, wizards can perform some pretty major mind tricks. Illusions trick others into seeing something that isn't really there. Comic book characters like Dr. Mist and The Wizard use mind tricks to fool their enemies. In *A Wizard of Earthsea*, Ged Sparrowhawk creates the illusion of fog to protect his city from raiders.

illusion: something that appears to be real but isn't

RISKY BUSINESS

Though wizards live in a fantasy-filled world, much of their magic is based on fact. To succeed and stay alive, wizards must understand how science works. Knowing which elemental attacks to use, such as fire or ice, is important when fighting enemies. A fire dragon would obviously be weak against water attacks but protected from flames.

Wizardry also has many rules, so a wizard who can't follow directions might be in big trouble. Without careful attention, their spells can go horribly wrong.

Ron Weasley

Want proof? Watch an episode of *Wizards of Waverly Place*. Giant zits and taxis come to life in strange and unexpected ways. Or look at Harry Potter's friend Ron Weasley. He tried to cast a spell with a broken wand. The curse backfired and Ron was throwing up slugs.

A wizard's weakness might be no different than yours.

Not all wizards are good, and nobody is totally protected. Some wizards even have limits to their magic. Some can only do a certain number of spells per day. They must choose wisely how to use their magic in battle. In some versions of the game Dungeons & Dragons, low-level wizards can cast just one attack spell each day.

Other wizards must be careful of curses. In the Harry Potter books, curses are used to kill, hurt, or hypnotize victims. During the Trinistyr Trilogy in the Dragonlance: The New Adventures series, Nearra must erase an ancient curse. The curse prevents her family from doing magic. No doubt about it—wizards have their work cut out for them!

HOCUS POCUS

Ever wish you could make it snow so that school would be canceled? Or maybe you're looking for a way to make your crush fall head over heels for you. Spells can do all of this and more. Some of the most common types include:

Spells of creation: Wizards might use spells to create objects out of thin air, like a bridge or a shield. Spells of illusion also fall under this category. Wizards can use them to create something that isn't really there. The spells can even change the way the wizard looks or make him invisible!

Spells of change: Change is a powerful thing, and spells can make it happen! With a change spell, a giant can become a dwarf—and vice versa. Wizards can also use these spells to turn people, objects, or animals into something else. Need to make a fast getaway?

No problem! Just turn yourself into a bird and fly away

Human or owl? You decide!

Spells of protection and destruction: These spells come in handy when danger is near. With these spells, wizards are able to create extreme weather conditions such as lightning or ice storms. They also make weapons such as fireballs or build walls to block enemies. These spells are also be used for protection against enemy spells.

Is this good or evil magic brewing?

22

Spells of enchantment: Enchantment spells are best used on people. From falling in love to falling asleep, these spells have very specific targets! Wizards can also use these spells to control what someone is thinking.

An enchanting spellcaster

✦ ✦ ✦ ✦ ✦ ✦ ✦ ✦ ✦ ✦ ✦ ✦ ✦ ✦ ✦ ✦ ✦ ✦

QUIZ: What's Your Spell Specialty?

A wizard's book of spells is way longer than any Harry Potter book. After all, the many types of spells are seemingly endless! So what spells would you be best at casting? Take this quiz, and you just might be spellbound by the results.

 When your little sis asks you for help, it's usually for:

a) playing a trick on friends
b) giving her a makeover
c) warding off bullies on the playground
d) giving her advice on her crush

 When it comes to your supernatural side, you identify most with:

a) wizards
b) witches
c) warlocks
d) fairies

 Your dream career would be:

a) artist
b) scientist
c) police officer
d) president

Which spell would you cast if you could?

a) making yourself invisible

b) transforming a rock into a diamond

c) creating a giant thunderstorm

d) turning an enemy into a friend

Your favorite Hogwarts teacher is:

a) Professor Lockhart

b) Professor McGonagall

c) Professor Moody

d) Professor Flitwick

Choose your familiar:

a) owl

b) black cat

c) dragon

d) snake

What's your wizardly tool of choice?

a) book of spells

b) wand

c) staff

d) potions

Look through your answers and see which letter you picked the most to reveal your spell specialty! If you circled:

Mostly As: What a clever trickster you are! Your spell specialties are creation and illusion.

Mostly Bs: Presto change-o! You create spells of change.

Mostly Cs: Your spells of protection and destruction are truly a force. Depending on the day, you can be someone's best friend or worst enemy!

Mostly Ds: Your enchantment spells are sure to charm.

25

✦ ✦ ✦ ✦ ✦ ✦ ✦ ✦ ✦ ✦ ✦ ✦ ✦ ✦ ✦ ✦

Chapter Four

Presto! Wizards in Pop Culture

Supporting Cast

From friends to foes, there is no shortage of magical characters in the wizarding world. So who can be found walking the halls of places like Hogwarts? Here are some of the most common groups:

Like wizards, witches practice **sorcery** and perform magic. Unlike wizards, they are usually female. Though witches can be good, some have the power to get in touch with evil spirits.

sorcery: magic that controls evil

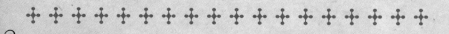

Witches On Screen: Hermione from the Harry Potter series, the White Witch in The Chronicles of Narnia, Selena Gomez as Alex Russo on *Wizards of Waverly Place*

Some elves love using their magic for mischief! Elves often come in two types—light and dark. Light elves are friendly and full of sunshine. Dark elves like to hide and are rarely spotted.

Elves On Screen: Legolas and Elrond from The Lord of the Rings, Dobby in *Harry Potter and the Chamber of Secrets*

Like elves, fairies are known as "fair folk." These dainty darlings love to fly about and spread their magic in nature. Sometimes they even shape-shift into butterflies, dragonflies, or other flying creatures.

Fairies On Screen: Tinkerbell from *Peter Pan*, The Fairy Godmother from *Shrek 2*

WIZARD YEARBOOK

Most Valuable Player
Harry Potter

Give this lovable wizard a wand or a broomstick, and he's sure to succeed!

Biggest Mischief-Maker:
Alex Russo

When not stirring up potions on *Wizards of Waverly Place*, Alex is usually stirring up mischief.

Best Team Players
Prue, Piper, Phoebe, and Paige Halliwell

These *Charmed* sisters are there to protect the innocent and take down evil.

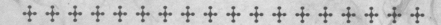

Most Backwards Mentor
Merlin

In The Once and Future King, Merlin lives through time backwards—he tells Arthur the future but gets confused about the past.

Darkest Wizard
Lord Voldemort

Whether ruling Hogwarts or plotting to take over the wizarding world, this bad guy is always up for a challenge.

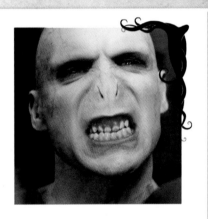

Most Inspiring Storyteller
J. R. R. Tolkien

The father of fantasy, this author is responsible for classics like The Lord of the Rings and The Hobbit.

GLOSSARY

apprentice (uh-PREN-tuhs)—someone who learns a trade or craft by working with a skilled person

enchant (en-CHANT)—to feel charmed or under the spell of magic

illusion (i-LOO-zhuhn)—something that appears to be real but isn't

mortal (MOR-tuhl)—someone or something that is not able to live forever; humans are mortal

potion (POH-shun)—a mixture of liquids thought to have magical effects

prediction (pri-DIK-shuhn)—a statement of what you think will happen in the future

shaman (SHAH-muhn)—a religious leader who uses magic

sorcery (SOR-sur-ee)—magic that controls evil spirits

trilogy (TRIL-uh-gee)—a series of three works that are closely related and develop a single theme

READ MORE

Kerns, Ann. *Wizards and Witches.* Fantasy Chronicles. Minneapolis, Minn.: Lerner Publications Company, 2010.

Steer, Dugald, ed. *The Wizardology Handbook: A Course for Apprentices: Being a True Account of Wizards, Their Ways, and Many Wonderful Powers as Told by Master Merlin.* Cambridge, Mass.: Candlewick Press, 2007.

INTERNET SITES

FactHound offers a safe, fun way to find Internet sites related to this book. All of the sites on FactHound have been researched by our staff.

Here's all you do:

Visit *www.facthound.com*

Type in this code: 9781429654548

INDEX